THE
PENNSYLVANIA
DUTCH
COOKBOOK

THE PENNSYLVANIA DUTCH COOKBOOK

by **Gerald S. Lestz**

Illustrations by
Walter Ferro

GROSSET & DUNLAP
A NATIONAL GENERAL COMPANY
Publishers · New York

A Castle Books, Inc. Edition
Distributed To The Trade
By Book Sales, Inc.

PREFACE

This book is an effort to catch some of the spirit of the Pennsylvania Dutch as well as the flavor of their food.

Many persons helped me, as evidenced by the credit lines on most of the recipes. Some were contributed anonymously.

Special credit goes to Mrs. John H. Brown of Meeting House Bluff, Marietta, Lancaster County, consultant-in-chief on recipes. A good cook, she has not only reviewed all of the recipes considered for this volume but provided a succulent cross section of her own recipes.

A local volume from which some of the recipes were drawn was *The Bookmobile Cook Book*, a one-copy collection, compiled by Miss M. Elinor Harsh during her service with the Lancaster Library.

Dr. Charles D. Spotts, an educator who is an authority on the Pennsylvania Dutch, kindly reviewed the historical material in this book.

Others who assisted in compilation and preparation included, Mrs. James O. Ament, Mrs. Harold E. Ruble and Miss Sara E. Fisher.

For anyone seeking additional information about the Pennsylvania Dutch or their food, we suggest works by Dr. John A. Hostetler, Professor Fredric Klees, J. George Frederick, Edna Eby Heller and Grant Stoltzfus and back issues of *Baer's Agricultural Almanac.*

Almanac House   Gerald S. Lestz
July 14, 1970

CONTENTS

THE
PENNSYLVANIA
DUTCH
COOKBOOK

I: AN INFORMAL HISTORY OF THE PENNSYLVANIA DUTCH

The peaceful setting of carefully tilled farms, green fields and pink orchards might lead visitors to Pennsylvania Dutch country into believing that here is a reincarnation of old-time America. But the land was not always so cultivated. It was once a wilderness that required men and women of courage and character to tame it.

The two main streams of German immigrants to Pennsylvania were the Anabaptists and the Lutherans and Reformed.

The Anabaptists—the Mennonites, Amish and others—were a religious sect of the Palatinate, a region of Bavaria. Because of their unorthodox religious beliefs they were subject to horrifying persecution.

Towns and villages were levelled; fields and barns were burned; robbery, killing and rape swept the countryside. In the Thirty Years' War, the population of the Palatinate was reduced from 500,000 to 50,000.

With the Treaty of Westphalia, some respite ensued but then Louis XIV of France ordered his armies into the Palatinate and the devastation began again. The waves of persecutions caused the Anabaptists to desperately search for a place where they could live in peace.

Meanwhile in England, where religious foment

was as strong if not as destructive as on the continent, William Penn had received his grant for a colony in the New World. Penn, actively seeking colonists, sent agents to the continent to spread the word of religious freedom in his new colony.

The Mennonites, impressed with Penn's political and religious views, decided to accept his offer. On October 6, 1683, thirteen Mennonite families sailed from Crefeld, where they had been employed as linen weavers. They sailed on the *Concord*, which might be called the Pennsylvania Dutch *Mayflower*, and landed at Philadelphia and founded Germantown.

The early arrivals faced many problems—they didn't speak English; they weren't British citizens; they were pacifists, and most important they had to start from scratch. The bitter winter of 1708-09 was a factor in the migration to the west of Philadelphia to present-day Lancaster County. Accounts of that winter say that birds froze in flight, animals died in their dens and men succumbed while walking. Through hard work and dedication the Anabaptists surmounted their difficulties and soon were sending word to their co-religionists to join them.

Thereafter migration grew, but impediments remained. The ships were poorly outfitted for the voyage that often required months. Raging storms, rocky coasts and illness took many lives. Some of the voyagers could not pay their fare and had to come as redemptioners, pledged to work five or seven years for anyone who would pay their voyage.

Members of Lutheran and Reformed churches started coming to Pennsylvania in the early 1700's, but they were not fleeing persecution because, in Europe, their churches were established. Economic hardship, the ravages of war and the harsh weather caused them to migrate to America.

These immigrants were not "Plain" people, as were the Amish and the Mennonites. They built their churches architecturally similiar to those in Europe in contrast to the Plain people who conducted prayer in members' homes or in austere meetinghouses.

To the Lutheran and the Reformed pioneers goes the credit for the Pennsylvania Dutch handicraft tradition, for much of the economic growth of the areas in which they settled and for a great amount of the inventiveness that made Pennsylvania products and customs an integral part of national development.

Moravians completed the settlement by migrating around 1740, primarily as missionaries to bring the Gospel to the Indians and aid congregations of other Protestant denominations, especially the Lutherans.

The Germanic tongue remained with the settlers even though they began to learn English in order to converse with the other settlers and to carry on business with the government. As the years went by, the Low German that was used conversationally became infiltrated with English terms. Predominantly German in vocabulary and inflection, it became a language all its own, known, of course, as Pennsylvania Dutch. This was not the

High German of the Bible or of the hymns they sang—it was the argot of the people.

This in turn affected the way persons of Germanic origin spoke English. Neighbors who did not speak the dialect found amusement in such expressions as "outen the light," or "spritz the grass" or "throw the cow some hay the fence over." Amusing or not, Pennsylvania Dutch persisted in use and is still the household and familiar language of Amish.

In addition to being skillful farmers, who tilled fertile lands that the English had passed by, the Pennsylvania Dutch showed ingenuity in industry, through invention, improvement and manufacture of useful—and attractive—products.

One of these was the rifle. Until the early eighteenth Century, rifles had a low degree of accuracy. The guns made by the Pennsylvania Dutch soon became known for their trueness. The guns were first used to bag game, an essential element in feeding a family.

In the French and Indian War, the guns were utilized against human targets. In the Revolutionary War, the guns became known among the British, whose numbers they reduced seriously, as "widow-makers."

This gun was the Lancaster Rifle. But since Daniel Boone, a native of Berks County, carried it onto the bloody ground of Kentucky, and the young nation came to associate it with exploits there, it became most widely known as the Kentucky Rifle.

Another great contribution of the Pennsylvania Dutch was the Conestoga wagon, a carefully constructed vehicle which moved freight and people and in its day was the major element in transportation in the Colonies.

The wagon originated in the Conestoga Valley of Lancaster County, in the very early years of the 18th Century—one record sets the date at 1716. It was a substantial and attractive vehicle, able to withstand the rigors of the roads, which were often barely more than trails, and highly decorative in appearance, with its white cloth cover, and red and blue body. It was red, white and blue before those became the national colors.

II THE AMISH TODAY

The Amish, of all the Pennsylvania Dutch settlers, are closest in custom to those of their ancestors. Over the years they have changed but their rate of change is slower than for any other Plain sect and, of course, even slower than the rate of change of the general populace.

The Amish are literal conservatives in the sense of preserving traditions and the traditional way of doing things, for example, riding horses and wagons rather than automobiles and doing without electricity. In still another way are the American Amish remarkable for their conservatism. They have preserved the faith of their fathers in the new land, while in Europe the Amish way of life has died out. In America the Amish have persistantly maintained their identity as unworldly nonconformists in a land where virtually all forces are drawing everyone into a homogeneous mold.

However, some forces are succeeding in making the Amish conform. One is economics—one of the pervading forces of life. It is a tradition with the Amish for the father to provide each son with a farm. In Pennsylvania, for example, this is impossible due to land shortage. Consequently some young men have sought occupation away from the shelter of the family farm. Some conduct small

16

business enterprises that are farm-related, such as buggy making, or take jobs in house building or related occupations that generally keep them within the home neighborhood. Others go into the outside world—they take factory jobs where they are surrounded by strangers, new customs and electrically operated machinery.

Those who do leave the family farm generally do well although some employers have been surprised when their Amish employees expect the day off to attend weddings and funerals. Ascension Day is a strict Amish holiday and no one is supposed to work. Legend tells women that if they sew on Ascension Day, lightning will strike them.

Amish women are beginning to work too, but the working woman is not as common among the Amish as in the general population. Most Amish men feel as American men did a half century ago, that the woman's place is in the home. But now a few Amish women are breaking out of that stricture. One young woman operates a very busy shop that stocks sewing and other household materials, near Intercourse, Pennsylvania. Another operates a gift shop and serves meals for visitors seeking Amish food. Another helps at a fruit stand in Central Market. Others work at a flower mart in Smoketown, or in a farm- and kitchen-oriented shop at Intercourse.

Amish girls are in demand as domestics and city women in the Pennsylvania Dutch territory consider themselves lucky to employ one. Families from big cities, outside the region, also seek these girls—but if metropolitan residents think they are going to get a simple miss who will work long hours for little pay, they are mistaken. The Amish, while hard and willing workers, will not be exploited.

While the Amish think the laborer deserves a living wage, they will have nothing to do with labor organizations. Union activity is relatively low throughout the Pennsylvania Dutch sects, and, in general, is not attractive to most workers in the region, even though bitter strikes have occurred.

The Amish are mainly farm dwellers. A few move into the smaller towns on retirement but most of the elders prefer the *gross dawdy-house* arrangement (gross dawdy means grandfather). When the parents become aged, they turn over the farm to a son, who lives in the main house. A dawdy-house is then built, usually connected to the larger house but still affording privacy for the older couple as well as the son and his family. The parents can continue to work on the farm and they are closely associated with the son's family—a family relationship that serves in many ways to maintain the strength of the Amish ties.

The strength of the family is extremely important for the maintenance—from one generation to the next—of the Amish way of life. It is especially significant in light of the many worldly attractions and temptations that intrude upon the Amish way of life and that would win more of their young away if the inner strength and adherence to tradition were not so well developed.

One of the questions most frequently asked, either of the Amish or of their neighbors, is whether many of their young people leave the fold and enter into a less circumscribed way of living. The answer to this is that the Amish have probably held on to far more of their children than any major faith in the United States. The exceptions are notable. Most often, if there is a break from the parental Old Amish roof, it is to a sect closely related, such as the House Amish or the Amish Mennonites or the Mennonites. The Old Order Mennonites are almost as conservative as the Amish. If a member leaves their church or commits a serious breach, the *meiding* or shunning is invoked.

The problem of teen rebellion, and teen participation in the modern sex revolution, is not as great among the Amish as among family groups in metropolitan centers. This is not to say that Amish young persons are dull carbon copies of their elders. They rebel and sow wild oats—displaying the impatience that has always been associated with youth—but very definitely in moderation.

The Amish were wearing long hair and beards long after they went out of style at the end of the Victorian era, and long before they came back into vogue in the 1960's. But their long hair is not a symbol of rebellion; it is merely a part of their nonconforming conservative way—and beards are grown only by married men.

Because of their upbringing, few Amish boys and girls take part in riots or sit-ins. They are not paper saints, however. When the boys get together at their own parties they let loose. The most hectic of these gatherings are the hootenannies held on farms about once a month during the summer. Usually, when the boys are holding a hootenanny the parents go away for the evening. Alcoholic beverages are drunk and non-Amish persons who have been present say things can get rather wild. Amish girls are sometimes present.

During the summer of 1969 one hootenanny in Chester County made splashy headlines when local police halted party-goers at the end of the evening. A large number of arrests were made and controversy erupted shortly thereafter when the defenders of the Amish youths charged that the policemen had no factual basis on which to lodge charges of intoxication.

The Amish "singing" is a far more orderly and more regularly scheduled type of get-together for the young men and girls. The singing is usually held in a barn or other large building, with boys seated on one side and girls on the other. They sing without instrumental accompaniment, either high-pitched German chorale hymns or more lively evangelistic music. Amish boys and girls often have their first dates at singings.

Courtship customs are far more fixed among the Amish than among the American youth in general. The buggy still predominates as the vehicle in which couples ride, and even though some Amish boys own and operate automobiles, their cars are usually older models, and not the sleek racing type. And the buggy has one advantage that no one-arm driver of a motor car can match. As in grandfather's day, "the horse knows the way" and a young Lothario need not devote his entire attention to driving when he has a sweet little Amish miss beside him. Buggy rules are just as fixed as all other customs of courting. An unmarried Amish boy always rides with the top down, in a phaeton-type vehicle. Only after marriage does an Amishman ride with the top up, or in a wagon that has a permanent top.

Boys and girls get together at occasions other than singings. Weddings of friends provide such opportunities; so do parties of a farm type, such as an "apple-schnitzing" (a party at which apples are peeled for drying and storage).

The ardent suitor also manages to see his girl on a Saturday night, fairly often. Custom says he should make his call after her parents are in bed. Whether the parents are sleeping or not, they give silent assent to his visit. He arrives as quietly as he can, and sends the beam of his flashlight to his girl's window. She tiptoes down and opens the door for him. This is a house date. The two are with each other several hours, either in the sitting room or in an upstairs bedroom.

Preparation for marriage, among the Amish girls, includes gathering of household objects they will need. The dower chest, primarily thought of as a charmingly painted Pennsylvania Dutch antique, has its counterpart today. Into it go glassware, china and linens.

As the Proverb said, to everything there is a season, so there is a wedding season for the Amish. This occurs in October and November, after the harvest has been gathered. The Court House in a country seat, such as Lancaster, York, Reading or Lebanon, becomes a focal point for the young couples as they enter to make and sign their applications.

Since about twenty family names predominate among the Amish, an application for a wedding license often shows frequent repetition of the same last name. One application, for example, was made by a girl named Stoltzfus and a boy named Stoltzfus. They were not related, even though the name was the same. And each had a Stoltzfus for a mother and a father—again, not related.

Most of the applicants are in the same age group —late teens, or early twenties. One seldom sees weddings for older single persons, although widows enter new unions, as do widowers. There are some Amish spinsters, but few confirmed Amish bachelors.

There is no period in Amish life equal to the "engagement" which is so much a part of the non-Amish culture. If a couple has decided to go "for steady," then it becomes accepted among their elders and peers that they plan to be married. Since the Amish do not wear jewelry, other than an occasional small pin, there is no engagement ring, and there is no wedding band.

The old idea of going to the girl's father to announce one's intentions, a custom that has generally disappeared in America, does have an Amish counterpart, except that the boy speaks to the bishop, who is the religious head of the neighborhood unit in which the girl lives. This is confidential and so is the bishop's conferring with the girl's father to learn if he approves. In most cases, papa says yes.

The wedding is held at the home of the bride, and follows a time-honored pattern. The bishop performs the ceremony, which takes several minutes but is preceded by a three-hour worship service. Feasting and singing go on all day. Guests sometimes come from a long distance and this is a time for exchanging news. In contrast to Western customs, the bride does not wear a long white gown with a veil. Her costume is a Sunday dress, in the same pattern as other dresses, but of a better material. It is handmade, of course. Favorite colors for the wedding dress are blue or purple, with a white cape and apron.

Food is important for the Amish wedding day. There are two major meals—noontime and evening—but there is also a table of food set up for informal sampling throughout the day.

Menus are traditional. Roasted fowl—chicken, duck or goose—is the entree for the noon meal. There are mashed potatoes with gravy, raw celery, cooked celery and other vegetables.

For the all-day food, a large table is placed in the center of the house, which has been opened up for the wedding. Sometimes a table is set in the kitchen. The young folks go in to sing at this table in the afternoon.

The evening meal usually consists of stewed chicken served over wafers. The wafers are either homemade or a commercial cracker such as Ritz. Fried sweet potatoes and peas or corn are staples.

At the bridal dinner, the newlyweds sit at the *eck* (corner) of the table with some unmarried friends. There is always special food for the bride's table, fried oysters, cakes, candies and fresh fruit. The young men who handle the horses and the girls who wait on the other tables are served from the bride's table.

The Amish "take care of their own." They do not go on relief when they run into financial misfortune; somehow their brethren rally around and quietly help them pay their bills. Their religious teachings prohibit them from buying or paying any kind of insurance—not only Social Security—but life, fire or theft, also.

Consequently, when fire destroys an Amish man's barn, it is a calamity from which he might not be able to extricate himself alone. That has brought about one of the most publicized of all the Amish activities—the barn-raising.

Why is it so appealing to outsiders? For one, it typifies the age-old custom of helping one another. Also, the barn is symbolic—the fruit of man's labor is in it; his livestock, his farm implements, his hay. But in addition, there is the fact that the building is erected in a single day, thereby rapidly providing a usable structure to replace one that was destroyed. The time element has a breathless air of unreality about it, made all the more unbelievable in this age where construction of a home takes so long—what with strikes; materials that fail to arrive on schedule, and plans that prove impracticable.

Perhaps above all else is the precision—the predesigning, the cutting and morticing of certain wooden parts in advance, and then the orderly fashion in which each man takes his place and dispatches his duties, until the framework is up, the roof and siding are on, and the interior is ready for finishing.

The barn-raising is normally preceded by an activity which is less dramatic to the visiting viewer, and probably less pleasure to the participant —cleaning up the debris left in the wake of the fire. But Amish men look on this as routine, and do not always limit this practice to the farms of their members. Several years ago in New Holland the Rubinson Department Store, founded by Samuel Rubinson and catering to Plain customers for nearly half a century, was destroyed by fire. Members of the Plain sects, headed by their bishops, volunteered and helped clear the lot.

Amish men will also travel halfway across the continent to help brethren in distress. One fine example was the trip many of the Amish made from the East, to help clear up an area in the mid-West after a tornado. Some stayed several weeks.

For a barn-raising, a key group of carpenters is chosen, a day is set and the helpers start arriving early in the morning. The men go about their appointed duties, while the women prepare food. People come and go through the day; horses and wagons arrive and depart; some spend a few hours, then go home and do chores, and return. The sounds of sawing and hammering are heard throughout the neighborhood.

Meal preparation is a job of heroic size. Mary Emma Showalter, in the *Mennonite Community Cook Book*, shows an old list of ingredients for a barn-raising dinner—115 lemon pies, 500 fat cakes (doughnuts), 16 chickens, 300 light rolls, 16 loaves bread, 5 gallons white potatoes and the same amount of sweet potatoes—and on and on. The bottom line on the recipe is the clincher: "Enough food for 175 men." And it was all prepared in one home kitchen!

By evening, the job is well enough along so that the full crew is no longer needed. The carpenters and the cooks depart, and the Amish family with the new barn can retire, happy in another demonstration of Amish brotherhood (and with enough food to last a week).

The barn-raising, in reality, is more symbolic than actual today. In a given county, if a dozen barns have to be replaced in a year, it's a lot. But the Amish stand ready; the old hands turn to and show their skill; the young hands learn the knack, and that's the way it goes on, from generation to generation.

RECIPES

Pennsylvania Dutch cookery was affected by many factors—weather, the background of the settlers, the food available. Most of the settlers came from the regions of Europe that are now Switzerland and Germany and Pennsylvania Dutch cuisine does tend to the hearty side with many starch dishes.

The harsh winters probably account for the early attempts of the Pennsylvania Dutch at dehydrating food, most notably "schnitz"—apples, cut into slices and dried that were stored in the attic and used throughout the winter, with the addition of water, for apple sauce, apple pie and other dishes.

Many of the recipes in this book date back to the open hearth when the fireplace was not only the source of heat and light but the oven, as well. Some are more recent and others have never been published or listed anywhere.

CURING HAM AT HOME

My husband's parents and grandparents cured their hams by this method and we still do. We have an old farm house with the old-fashioned dirt-floor cellar. It has the natural dampness that is absolutely necessary to cure hams—without it the ham would spoil. We have been curing hams like this for fourteen years and never has one spoiled.
—Mrs. Robert D. Strauss

---

30 pounds salt	½ teaspoon salt
3 tablespoons pepper	peter
2 pounds sugar	Patent smoke

Enough for 2 fresh hams and 2 shoulders. Mix the first four ingredients thoroughly in a wooden tub. Rub hams and shoulders with mixture. Lay on meat bench in cellar. Cover with the leftover salt mixture and leave for 4 weeks. Wipe off salt and hang meat in the attic. About a week later wipe or brush on patent smoke. Repeat the brushing 2 weeks later. Cover with muslin bags and tie shut. Let hang until Easter (Butchering is done in the fall and hams hung then) and they are ready to eat.

TO CURE PORK

· `Frank Fyock

10 quarts salt	½ pound salt
4 pounds black	peter
pepper	2 ounces red
4 pounds brown	pepper
sugar	Lukewarm water

Enough for 1,000 pounds of meat. Mix ingredients thoroughly. Add water to make a paste. Spread on meat morning and evening for 3 days. Lay on a bench to drain. When drained, hang.

ROAST PIG'S STOMACH

—*Mrs Arthur Ebhert*

1 pig's stomach	2 cups of diced
1 pound fresh	bread
sausage	1 tablespoon
2 to 3 quarts	parsley flakes
diced raw	Salt
potatoes	Pepper

Clean the pig's stomach thoroughly. Mix the remaining ingredients and fill stomach. Close both ends by sewing shut with needle and cord or by using poultry nails and cord. Bake for around 3 hours or until well done. Keep some water in the pan while roasting. Serve with sweet potatoes, cranberries and pumpkin pie.

STUFFED HOG MAW

A Pennsylvania Dutchman is a frugal person who will make use of everything. My grandfather was a farmer who raised pigs and at butchering time every conceivable part of the animal was utilized. Sutffed hog maw (pig's stomach) probably originated in Germany.
—Mrs. Robert C. Neiman

1 medium-sized hog maw	2 pounds bulk pork sausage meat
4 cups diced raw potatoes	1 teaspoon salt
2 cups grated cabbage	

Wash and clean hog maw inside and out with cold water. Sew shut the thick end with a heavy needle and cord. Mix remaining ingredients thoroughly and pack loosely into the maw. Sew the remaining opening shut. Place in a roaster on a rack, adding enough water to cover bottom of pan. Cover tightly with a lid and bake for 4 to 5 hours at 325°. If a crisp skin is preferred, bake a little longer. Garnish with parsley and crabapples. This dish can be served with fruit, usually crabapples, or with orange gelatin and peach halves—and of course, cole slaw. *Serves 4.*

MINCEMEAT

This recipe for mincemeat has been in the family for several generations. I would guess it dates back to the early 1800's. It is a bit different in that the beef is cooked only once, at the time of baking, which, in our opinion, makes it taste a lot better.
—*Mrs. Henry Walter, Jr.*

2 pounds round steak, freshly ground
1 pound suet, mixed with beef
2 pounds brown sugar
2 pounds seedless raisins
2 quarts apples, pared and ground
1 pint blended whiskey

Take a large dishpan and put all of the ingredients in together and mix thoroughly with your hands. Store in pint jars in the refrigerator for about a week before freezing. When making pies add cinnamon and ½ cup more whiskey. Bake at 400° for about 40 minutes or until brown.

SUSQUEHANNA HASH

During the Depression a group of us were fishing along the Susquehanna river north of Harrisburg each in turn doing the cooking for the group with whatever provisions we could afford to buy or what we could beg from the neighborhood farmers.

After several days of camping, provisions started to run low and my brother, whose turn it was to cook, took stock of what was on hand. A piece of slab bacon, a few onions, a few potatoes, some eggs and two cans of pork and beans. Not liking to wash pots and pans, my brother decided to put it all together in one skillet and, thus, a new but filling meal was invented.
—Carroll R. Allwein

Bacon	**Eggs**
Onions	**Pork and beans**
Cooked potatoes	**Shortening (optional)**

Fry the bacon using other shortening or oil if there is not enough fat, brown the onions till about golden. Slice cooked potatoes and add to pan, cook till done. Slightly beat the eggs and pour over the mixture, keep turning until the eggs are lightly fried and then add pork and beans. Keep turning until the beans are well heated and you have a meal to satisfy any healthy appetite be it growing child or robust farmer.

Make it in small or large amounts, using as much of each ingredient to suit your taste. I have used it for three people and also for a whole troop of Boy Scouts and they always cleaned out the skillet and looked for more.

SCHNITZ UN KNEPP

—*Mrs. Robert Gross, Sr.*

1 quart dried apples	¼ teaspoon pepper
1 3-pound ham	4 teaspoons baking powder
2 tablespoons brown sugar	1 egg, well beaten
2 cups flour	Milk
1 teaspoon salt	3 tablespoons melted butter

Pick over and wash dried apples (schnitz). Cover with water and let soak overnight. In morning, cover ham with cold water and boil for 3 hours.

Add the apples and water in which they have been soaked and continue to boil for another hour. Add brown sugar. Make dumplings (knepp) by sifting together the flour, salt, pepper and baking powder. Stir in the beaten egg, milk (enough to make moist but stiff batter) and butter. Drop the batter by small spoonfuls into the hot liquid with the ham and apples, cover kettle tight and cook dumplings for 15 minutes. Serve piping hot on large platter. Sometimes I leave the lid off till they boil, then put on lid.

BAKED CHICKEN PIE

—Mrs. Charles L. Wagner

Chicken (preferably, one year old)	Chopped parsley
	Pastry dough
	Diced potatoes
1 cup cream or rich milk	Minced onions
	Finely diced celery
Flour	
1 or 2 hard-cooked egg yolks	

Boil chicken until tender. Remove from bones and cut into bite-sized pieces. Add cream (or milk) to the chicken broth, bring to a boil and thicken with flour paste. Boil several minutes, then crumble egg yolks into the gravy, also add chopped parsley. Keep hot after adding chicken meat.

Prepare your favorite pastry recipe. Roll out to the thickness of about 3/16 of an inch. Pierce with fork, cut pastry into squares and bake on a cookie sheet. Pare and dice white potatoes. Cook in salt water with onions and celery until vegetables are soft.

To serve, have chicken and gravy, hot pastry and vegetables in separate dishes or platters. Have each person help themselves first to a few squares of pastry, then potatoes over pastry and chicken and gravy over potatoes with room for pastry on top.

OLD-FASHIONED BAKED BEANS

—Mrs. Mervin M. Hess

1 **pound navy beans**	½ **cup brown sugar**
1 **onion, finely chopped**	¾ **cup catsup**
¾ **cup molasses**	½ **pound bacon, cut in small pieces**

Soak beans in cold water overnight. Drain, add 2½ quarts fresh water in the morning. Cook slowly until soft, approximately 1½ hours. When the skins burst they are soft enough. Drain, place in a large cake pan and add the rest of the ingredients. Mix well and bake at 350° for ½ hour or until brown. These should be very moist; if necessary, add some of the liquid you boiled the beans in.

POTATO SLICES

These are an adaptation of the slices that were made on the top plates of the old cook stove. They are great for snacks or supper.
—Mrs. John H. Brown

Wash and slice potatoes into ¼-inch slices. Place in a 400° oven and bake for ½ hour. If not blistered and brown, place under broiler until brown. Butter and salt and eat with fingers. These need not be put in a pan or in foil —just place on the rack in the oven.

BAUER KNEPP

This recipe is very, very old. It was the stand-by of pioneers traveling on foot or otherwise. Their store usually consisted of flour meal, salt and bacon. They mixed the flour, salt and hot water and fried the cakes in bacon fat. Serving with milk and sugar was left for those who owned a cow and could buy sugar.
—Mrs. Charles C. Wagner

½ teaspoon salt
3 cups stone-
    ground flour
Boiling water

Shortening
Milk
Sugar

Mix salt and flour. Slowly pour hot water over flour while stirring. Pour just enough hot water so that flour clings together but is still rather dry. Heat shortening in a heavy pan. Put tablespoons of dough in hot fat and press down flat to ½ inch or less. Fry until golden brown. Turn and brown other side. When all of the batch is finished, serve in flat soup dishes with milk and sugar. This sounds terrible but is delicious and chewy.

RAW POTATO CAKES

—*Mrs. Earl Singer*

2 **eggs**	2 **tablespoons**
2 **cups grated**	**flour**
raw potatoes	**Chopped**
1 **teaspoon**	**onion (op-**
salt	**tional)**

Beat eggs and add potatoes and salt. Stir in flour and onion. Form into patties and fry in hot fat. Turn to brown on both sides.

SUGAR PEAS & NEW POTATOES

—*Mrs. Albert L. Elko*

Cook both peas and (peeled) potatoes together (about a quart of peas to 1½ pounds new potatoes) until potatoes are cooked enough to your liking. Add your favorite cream sauce and you are finished. If any leftover cooked ham is around add it and you have a complete dinner. Chicken or beef could be used also.

NEW PEAS AND POTATOES

A delightful early summer dish.
—Mrs. Ervin C. Brown

3 cups fresh peas	1½ teaspoons salt
12 small new potatoes, skinned	Milk
	2 tablespoons melted butter
	1½ teaspoons flour

Cook peas and potatoes separately, in salt water until soft and almost dry. Add peas to potatoes. Pour milk over them and heat to boiling point, blend melted butter and flour and add slowly to hot vegetables cooking until slightly thick. Serves 6.

DRIED CORN

—Ruth M. Neff

9 cups fresh corn	½ cup milk
½ cup brown sugar	Pinch of salt

Mix ingredients and put in kettle. Simmer, stirring occasionally, till it is boiled dry. Then spread it in pans and dry in a slow oven or on a corn dryer.

POKE

Poke can be found in the woods and areas that aren't cultivated. I usually find it about the first week of June and gather it up until the time it blooms. Do not use poke after it blooms.
—*Mrs. Harold A. Williams*

3 cups poke	**1 teaspoon salt**
3 slices bacon	**2 teaspoons butter**
2 tablespoons vinegar	

Strip most of the leaves from the poke stalks and cut in 2-inch pieces, cook in lots of water until tender. Pour off the water, add a little more and simmer about 20 minutes more. Fry the bacon, crumble in small pieces. Take up in serving dishes, top with butter, bacon and pour the vinegar over. Serves 2.

FRIED PUMPKIN

This is a very old recipe. I was told by the older people in this area that they fried pumpkins to take the place of meat, which was very scarce.
—Mrs. Palmer Deppen

1 neck pumpkin	**Salt and pepper**
Milk	**½ cup flour**
1 egg	

Get a long-necked pumpkin. Peel the pumpkin and slice it very thin. Make a mixture of milk, egg, salt and pepper. Dip the pumpkin in the mixture and roll in flour. Fry slowly in shortening until brown.

EGG CHEESE I

My mother fed this dish to her family of thirteen because it was nutritious as well as economical. She would also take it to market and was one of the few stand-holders to sell it in the Arcade market in Lancaster.
—Mrs. Clayton S. Groff

2 quarts milk	**1 teaspoon salt**
4 eggs	**½ teaspoon sugar**
2 cups sour milk	

Bring sweet milk to boiling point. Beat eggs lightly, add sour milk, salt and sugar. Beat again. Pour mixture slowly into sweet milk. Cover and let stand for several minutes. Stir slowly until it separates.

Remove cheese from whey by using a ladle or spoon with holes. Put the cheese into a mold with holes. (It is very important that the mold have holes to allow for draining.)

Let set overnight or 8 hours. When set, unmold and serve with molasses or syrup.

EGG CHEESE II

—E. H. E.

2 quarts milk	**2 cups buttermilk**
5 eggs	**or sour milk**

Heat milk to boiling point. While milk is heating, beat eggs thoroughly and add buttermilk or sour milk to eggs, mixing well. Stir the egg mixture slowly into the hot milk and stir until it curdles enough to separate the cheese from the whey. Remove the curd from the whey and place curd into a cheese mold or into a strainer lined with a thin white cloth to give shape to the cheese. Chill and invert on plate to serve.

MOTHER'S BREAD STUFFING

My husband, who is not a Pennsylvanian, really likes this. My friends do too and find it different. I use this recipe whenever I can although saffron isn't as readily available in stores around the country as it is in Pennsylvania. When I do have saffron I save it for special occasions.
—Mrs. Roger Haseltine

Pinch of saffron mixed with 1 tablespoon boiling water	2 cups bite-sized pieces day-old bread
1 egg	1 onion, chopped
1 cup water or milk	2 stalks celery, chopped

Mix the saffron water with the egg and water or milk. Moisten bread in this mixture. In a frying pan brown the onion and celery, add the bread and brown slightly, turning as it browns. After browning, cool. It is ready for stuffing your turkey or just put in a casserole for reheating.

POTATO FILLING I

This Pennsylvania Dutch recipe is quite popular in Berks County (Reading area) but practically unknown in Lancaster County.
—Mrs. Robert C. Smith

2 cups hot
mashed
potatoes
1 egg, well beaten
1 quart fresh
bread crumbs
1 tablespoon
minced parsley

1 small onion,
minced
½ cup diced celery
2 tablespoons
melted butter
1 teaspoon salt
Pinch of pepper

Mix potatoes and egg. Soak bread in cold water and squeeze dry. Add to potato mixture. Stir in other ingredients and mix well. Put lightly in buttered casserole and bake until dry and lightly browned, about 30 minutes at 325-350°. *Serves 6.*

POTATO FILLING II
—*Mrs. Charles L. Beam*

2 loaves bread,
cut up and dried
8 eggs, well
beaten
10 or 12 large
boiled potatoes
1 teaspoon salt
1 teaspoon
pepper

½ teaspoon onion
salt
1 tablespoon
parsley
2 handfuls cut-up
celery
1 quart milk
Butter

Mix first 8 ingredients thoroughly. Put in a buttered 16x7x5-inch butcher pan. Dab top with butter. Bake at 350° for approximately 60 minutes. Serves 6.

FRIED BREAD FILLING

As a child I loved to visit my grandparents—especially if I could stay for a meal. My grandfather was a blacksmith, therefore the meals were hearty—the stick-to-the-ribs type. I enjoyed being there when my grandmother served Fried Bread Filling. As a matter of fact, if I could do it without being noticed, I ate nothing else. Naturally this is one of my favorite old recipes and I still serve it in place of potatoes, rice, noodles, etc.
—Mrs. Elmer Z. Delp

1 **large loaf fresh bread**	2 **cups milk**
1 **cup chopped onion**	½ **teaspoon saffron boiled for two minutes in**
1 **cup chopped celery**	½ **cup water**
1 **cup chopped parsley**	1 **teaspoon salt**
6 **eggs**	¼ **teaspoon fresh ground pepper**
	¼ **pound butter or margarine**

Cut each slice of bread into approximately 16 cubes. Place bread, raw onions, celery and parsley in large container. Beat eggs very well (either with an electric mixer or blender), add milk, saffron and water, salt and pepper and continue to mix until thoroughly blended.

Pour liquid ingredients over bread mixture and blend well. The old-fashioned method of using the hands seems to work best. The mixture should be quite moist.

Melt butter in large frying pan. Pour in bread mixture and fry slowly, turning frequently for 30 to 40 minutes.

RIVELS I

—*Mrs. Janet Canan*

To 2 tablespoons flour add 1 egg. Mix and add flour until it crumbles and falls apart. Add to soups and boil 5 or 6 minutes.

RIVELS II

—*Mrs. Morgan Medlar*

To 1 cup flour add 1 egg and a dash of salt. Mix thoroughly until it crumbles. Add to soups.

BREAD SOUP

½ to ¼ loaf bread	1 quart fresh
1 quart milk	or canned
Sugar to taste	strawberries or
	peaches

Break bread into bite-sized pieces in large bowl. Add milk and sugar to taste. Add whole berries or peach halves. *Serves* 4.

BEEF RIVEL SOUP

This is delicious. I remember Mother making this usually when she had a busy day and didn't have much time to make a big meal.
—Mrs. Donald E. Harnish

1 quart beef broth	**½ cup flour**
½ teaspoon salt	**¼ cup milk**
1 egg	

Heat broth and add salt. Make rivels by rubbing egg and flour together, then add milk. Drop rivels, which should be about the size of a cherry pit, into the hot broth. Boil for about 5 minutes, stirring occasionally. Serves 4.

PRETZEL SOUP

—Mrs. John H. Brown

Heat milk, add salt, pepper and gobs of butter. Pour into bowls. Add broken pretzels and serve.

46

WARM DRESSING FOR LETTUCE

—Mrs. Willard Trupe

3 strips bacon
1 egg, beaten

4 tablespoons
  vinegar
4 tablespoons sugar

Fry bacon slowly until brown and crisp. Drain and crumble bacon. Add to mixture of egg, vinegar and sugar. Heat until mixture boils or thickens. Fold lightly over lettuce.

POTATO SALAD DRESSING

—Mrs. Joan Way

2 eggs
1 tablespoon
  mustard
1 cup sugar

½ cup vinegar
½ cup water
Flour

Beat eggs and mustard together. Add sugar, vinegar and water. Stir to mix. Bring to a boil. Let boil about 8 minutes. Thicken with a little flour and water as you would for gravy.

Remove this dressing from fire and add it to cooked, diced potatoes mixed with celery, onions and hard-cooked eggs. Add salt and pepper for taste.

BACON GRAVY

This is a very old recipe used often when stored food was scarce at the end of winter.
—*Mrs. Charles C. Wagner*

Brown bacon snips in ham and remove pieces to a plate. Add flour to fat in pan, stir until smooth. Add hot water slowly to flour until you have a smooth gravy as thick or thin as you like. Boil several minutes then add a tablespoon of vinegar. Serve over potatoes in the jackets or with buttered string beans.

SOFT PRETZELS

This is a very old recipe and a surprising one. Who would ever think of boiling soft pretzels in baking soda water before baking?
—*Mrs. John H. Brown*

1 envelope yeast	Butter as needed
Pinch of sugar	4 teaspoons baking
2 teaspoons salt	soda
4 to 5 cups flour	Coarse salt for
	sprinkling

Dissolve yeast in ¼ cup warm water, then stir in an additional cup warm water and sugar. Pour yeast mixture into bowl and add salt. Beat in flour to make stiff dough. Knead for 10 minutes (until dough is elastic). Place in bowl and spread with butter. Cover. Let rise for 45 minutes or until double in bulk. Shape pretzels into sticks or twists. (Make into ½ thickness of desired pretzel). Bring 4 cups of water to boil with baking soda. Drop 3 pretzels in at a time and boil for 1 minute or until they float on surface. Remove and drain. Place on buttered cookie sheet. Sprinkle with salt. Bake in 475° oven about 12 minutes or until golden brown. Remove from sheet and place on rack.

CHICKEN WAFERS

This recipe comes from my paternal grandmother. Chicken wafers are a rich delicacy my four sisters and I would munch by the handfuls if mother didn't hide them. Eat them as a snack, or pour chicken broth over them in a dish.
—Mrs. Allen Fisher

4 cups flour	½ cup lard or
2 teaspoons	⅔ cup vegetable
baking powder	shortening
1 teaspoon salt	1 egg
	Milk

Combine flour, baking powder and salt. Cut in shortening (lard is preferred because it imparts a special old-fashioned flavor), then stir in the egg and enough milk to make a stiff dough. Roll out on cooky sheets, ⅛- to ¼-inch thick. Cut into small squares and bake at 400° until crisp and brown.

CUP CUSTARD

During World War I, we lived in Hershey, Pennsylvania. My mother opened a boarding house because the chocolate factory was growing and everyone was flocking to Hershey for jobs. She became so famous for her good cooking that doctors would stop and ask if they and their chauffeurs could eat dinner there. This is her egg custard recipe that she baked fresh every morning.
—Mrs. Floyd Witner

1 **cup granulated sugar**	4 **eggs**
1 **tablespoon flour**	3 **cups milk**
	⅓ **cup cream**

Mix sugar and flour. Add eggs, milk and cream and beat by hand. Pour into a large unbaked pie shell and bake at 375° until set. Remove from oven while still shaky—do not overbake.

GET-WELL CUSTARD

This was always given to us, as children, when we were "getting better" or on the road to recovery. It makes a good dessert—a little more substantial than jello. Always made in our best punch cups.
—Mrs. John H. Brown

1	package plain	1	cup light cream
	gelatin	1	cup milk
2	tablespoons sugar		Vanilla

Soften gelatin in plain milk. Mix sugar, cream, milk and gelatin and heat until gelatin is dissolved. Add vanilla. Pour into punch or custard cups and chill until firm and set.

CRACKER PUDDING

—Edith Landis Herr

½	cup sugar	1	cup shredded
2	eggs, separated		coconut
1	quart milk	1	teaspoon
2	cups soda		vanilla
	cracker crumbs	4	tablespoons
			sugar

Mix sugar and two egg yolks. Heat milk to boiling point. Add a few table-spoons hot milk to egg yolks. Beat egg yolk mixture into hot milk stirring constantly. Stir in cracker crumbs and coconut. Bring to boil for 1 or 2 minutes. Add vanilla. Pour into buttered baking dish. Prepare meringue by beating egg whites until stiff and adding sugar. Spread meringue on pudding and bake at 350° until golden brown.

SUET PUDDING

—Mrs. F.G. Fisher

1 cup suet ground through a food chopper
1 cup thick buttermilk
1 cup molasses
1 teaspoon soda
1 cup seedless raisins
¾ cup candied cherries
¾ cup candied pineapples
1 teaspoon cinnamon
½ teaspoon ground cloves
2 eggs, unbeaten
2¾ cups pastry flour
½ teaspoon salt

Mix all together. Place in greased bowls and steam 2½ to 3 hours. Serve hot with the following sauce.

Sauce:

3 cups water
2 tablespoons butter
¼ teaspoon salt
3 tablespoons cornstarch
¼ cup sugar
½ cup water

Bring 3 cups water, butter and salt to a boil. Add cornstarch, sugar and additional ½ cup water for thickening and boil together. Add more sugar or honey to taste. Serve hot on pudding.

BAKED RICE PUDDING

⅓ cup rice   ⅓ cup sugar
4 cups milk   Grated rind ½
½ teaspoon salt   lemon

Wash rice, mix with other ingredients, pour into a greased pudding dish, set in pan of hot water and bake in slow oven (300°) for 3 hours. Stir every 10 minutes during the first hour of baking to prevent rice from settling. *Serves 6.*

Chocolate Rice Pudding:

Use the above recipe, adding 1 square melted chocolate, 1 teaspoon vanilla and ½ teaspoon salt. Omit the lemon rind.

DUTCH PUDDING
(Apple or Cherry)

—*Mrs. W.C. Tennis*

1 egg	1 teaspoon salt
½ cup sugar	1 pint flour
1½ tablespoons butter	¾ cup milk
2 teaspoons baking powder	1 cup sour cherries or diced apples

Beat egg, add sugar and shortening and stir. Sift together baking powder, salt and flour; add alternately with milk. Stir in gently a cup of apples or cherries whichever is desired. Bake in a loaf pan, for 35 to 40 minutes, at 350°.

CHERRY PUDDING

—*Mrs. John P. Mohn*

2 eggs	1 teaspoon baking powder
½ cup milk	1½ cups flour
1 tablespoon melted butter	2 pounds pitted sour cherries (or peaches)
½ teaspoon salt	Sugar

Break eggs in a bowl and beat with hand beater. Add milk, butter and dry ingredients in that order. Put the batter in either an 8x 10-inch pan or two 8-inch round cake pans. Over the top put 2 pounds of pitted sour cherries. Canned fruit may be used if it is drained. Press the fruit into the batter and sprinkle with sugar. Bake at 350° for 40 minutes. Serve with milk and sugar.

PLUM PUDDING

A traditional holiday dish.
—Mrs. James O. Ament

1½ cups flour	1 teaspoon baking soda
1 teaspoon cloves	1 cup raisons
1 teaspoon cinnamon	1 cup currants
1 egg	1 cup bread crumbs soaked
1½ cups sugar	in 1½
4 tablespoons butter	cups milk

Mix ingredients together and pour into a tube pan. Steam for 1½ hours on top of the stove (in Dutch oven or large covered pot). Serve with the following sauce.

Sauce:

1 quart milk	Brown sugar
1 tablespoon cornstarch	Vanilla

Dissolve cornstarch in a little milk. Mix with the quart of milk and bring to a boil. Sweeten to taste with brown sugar and vanilla. The cake can be made the day before and resteamed.

BAKED APPLE PUDDING

—Mrs. Frank Reser

4 apples
Sugar
Cinnamon
1 pint flour
2 teaspoons baking
  powder

½ teaspoon salt
½ cup sugar
1 egg, well beaten
2 tablespoons
  melted lard
⅔ cup milk

Pare, core and slice apples and cover bottom of 1-inch deep baking dish. Sprinkle with sugar and cinnamon. Add a little water and cover with batter made by mixing the other ingredients. Bake ½ hour. Cherries or peaches can be substituted.

MORAVIAN MINTS

—Mrs. Willis H. Bucher

1 pound
  confectioners'
  sugar
5 teaspoons water

6 drops
  peppermint or
  wintergreen oil

Melt sugar with water before putting over boiling water in a double boiler. Boil sugar and water until it forms a skin on the top, then take off fire, add the oil. Drop right away on waxed paper.

STRAWBERRY PRESERVES

—*Agnes Rutler*

1 pint strawberries	**½ pint water**
	1½ pints sugar

Boil strawberries and water together for 10 minutes. Add sugar and boil an additional 30 minutes. Put in jars and seal.

GRANDMA'S CHRISTMAS BISCUITS

Old-fashioned cut-out cookies. These are thick and good for dunking.
—*Mrs. John H. Brown*

½ pound butter	**1 teaspoon cream of tartar**
1 pound granulated sugar	**1 teaspoon baking soda dissolved in small amount hot water**
1 cup sweet milk	**Flour**

Cream butter and beat in sugar, milk, tartar and baking soda. Add enough flour to enable batter to be rolled out and cut after being chilled all night. Bake at 375° for 15 minutes.

GRANDMA'S CHOCOLATE CRACKERS

A Christmas favorite.
—Mrs. John H. Brown

½ **pound brown sugar**	4 **eggs**
½ **pound granulated sugar**	1 **pound flour**
½ **pound butter**	½ **teaspoon baking soda**
	¼ **pound melted chocolate**

Cream sugars, butter and eggs. Add chocolate, flour and baking soda. Chill overnight and roll paper thin. Cut into designs with cookie cutters and bake at 300° for 8 minutes.

SHORTCAKE-SODA BISCUITS

Grandmother often baked shortcakes in an iron skillet on top of a hot stove, turning when brown on one side. All of her family liked to cut these cakes in half and plaster butter and mild molasses on them.
—Mrs. Charles L. Wagner

2 **cups sifted all-purpose flour**	4 **tablespoons shortening**
½ **teaspoon baking soda**	¾ **cup thick milk or buttermilk**
½ **teaspoon salt**	

Mix flour, soda and salt. Cut in shortening as for pie dough. Add enough milk to crumbs to make a soft dough and knead lightly a few times so it can be lightly rolled or patted ½-inch thick on flour board. Cut into squares. Bake on greased cookie sheet at 475° about 12 minutes or until brown.

AMISH SHOO FLY PIE

This recipe was given to me by my mother who in turn received it from an Amish woman who has a stand at the Berks County Farmers Market.
—*Mrs. Evelyn Mae Shaub*

1½ cups sifted flour	¾ cup boiling water
½ cup brown sugar, packed firmly	¾ cup dark molasses
¼ cup butter	½ teaspoon baking soda

Mix flour, sugar and butter till crumbly. Combine water, molasses and baking soda and pour into a 9-inch unbaked pie shell. Mix with crumbs, starting with the liquid and ending with the crumbs. Bake for approximately 30 minutes at 375°.

SHOO FLY PIE I

—Mrs. Ralph J. Gable

3 level cups flour	1 cup molasses
1 cup brown sugar	1 cup boiling water
¾ cup butter and lard	½ teaspoon baking soda
1 teaspoon baking powder	3 unbaked pie shells

Mix flour, sugar, shortening and baking powder into crumbs and reserve about ½ cup of crumbs to sprinkle over top of pie. Mix remaining ingredients and pour over crumbs and mix lightly. Line pie plates with unbaked pie crusts and pour in mixture. Sprinkle top with reserved dry crumbs. Bake.

SHOO FLY PIE II

—Mrs. Paul Kissinger

1 cup molasses	1 cup hot water
½ teaspoon cinnamon	3 cups flour
1 teaspoon vanilla	1 cup sugar
1 teaspoon baking soda	½ cup shortening, half butter or margarine

Put molasses in bowl, add cinnamon and vanilla. Dissolve soda in hot water and add to mixture. Pour into pie plates evenly. Mix flour, sugar and shortening with the hands until crumbly. Sprinkle evenly over molasses. Bake at 375° for about 45 minutes.

SHOO FLY PIE III

This is a recipe I have carried with me to Baltimore and now to Venezuela where it was contributed to a cookbook put together by a local women's organization.
—Mrs. Mary Sequi

4 cups flour	1 cup water
2 cups sugar	1 teaspoon ginger,
½ cup shortening	or ½ teaspoon
1 teaspoon	cinnamon and ½
baking soda	teaspoon ginger
1 cup molasses	Pinch of baking
	soda

Take the first four ingredients and mix into crumbs. Mix molasses, water, ginger and soda and pour into two unbaked pie shells. Divide crumbs on the top of each pie. Bake at 375° for about 1 hour.

STRAWBERRY PIE

My mother always took great pride in making the meals very attractive in looks and in taste. Among her favorite pie recipes is this straw-berry pie, which she has passed out to many of her friends. She is blind now, but she still loves to cook and hear new recipes.
—Mrs. John Mumma

1	baked pastry shell	3	tablespoons cornstarch
1	quart strawberries	1	cup whipping cream
1	cup granulated sugar		

Select the choicer half of the strawberries and place in a baked pie shell. Mash the remaining berries until the juice is well extracted. Mix sugar and cornstarch, bring juice to a boil and add the cornstarch and sugar mixture. Cook slowly for about 10 minutes, stirring occasionally. Let cool and pour over the uncooked berries in the pastry shell. Place the pie in the refrigerator until very cold. Top with sweetened whipped cream and serve.

FUNERAL PIE I

The Amish serve these only for funerals.
—Mrs. Harold A. Miles

1 cup seeded raisins, washed	2 tablespoons grated lemon rind
1½ cups sugar	Juice of a lemon
4 tablespoons flour	Pinch of salt
1 egg, well beaten	

Soak raisins for 3 hours in water. Mix sugar, flour and egg. Add rind, juice, salt and raisins. Cook in double boiler for 15 minutes, stirring occasionally. When the mixture is cool, pour the mixture into a dough-lined pie plate. Cover raisins with a lattice top. Bake pie in oven at 400° for about 40 minutes or until nice and brown.

FUNERAL PIE II

—Mrs. Earl Singer

1 cup raisins	Juice of a lemon
½ cup sugar	4 tablespoons flour
1 egg	

Soak raisins in water for about 2 hours. Mix other ingredients, put in unbaked pie crust. Bake for 35 minutes at 350°. Test with toothpick.

SOUR CREAM RAISIN PIE

—*Mrs. Grace Strickler*

1 tablespoon flour	1 cup sugar
½ teaspoon cinnamon	2 eggs
½ teaspoon nutmeg	1½ cups sour cream
	1½ cups raisins

Mix flour, spices and sugar. Add eggs, sour cream and raisins. Bake in an unbaked pastry shell for about 30 minutes at 360°.

SCHNITZ PIE

These pies are made especially for Amish weddings. When they are baked they make one to two hundred. November is the month to get married and the days are usually Tuesday or Thursday.

—*Mrs. Morris Coffroad*

1 pound of schnitz (dried apples)	2 tablespoons cinnamon
1 orange, rind and juice	Prepared pie crust
2 cups sugar	Butter

Cover schnitz with water and soak overnight. Add orange rind and juice and more water if necessary. Boil until soft, then put through colander and add sugar and cinnamon. Pour into pastry-lined shell, dot with butter, cover with top crust or lattice strips.

Bake in hot oven (450°) for 10 minutes. Reduce to 350° and bake 30 minutes.

UNION PIE

—Mrs. Grace Strickler

2 cups sugar	½ cup water
4 tablespoons flour (heaping)	1 teaspoon baking soda
1 teaspoon cinnamon	1 cup thick milk
2 eggs	1 cup sour cream

Mix sugar, flour and cinnamon, add eggs and water and mix well. Dissolve soda in a little thick milk, add thick milk and cream. Don't beat after you put in the milk and cream, just mix a little. Bake in an unbaked pie shell till set or an inserted silver knife comes out clean.

LEMON SPONGE PIE

—Alma Mylin

1 cup granulated sugar	¼ teaspoon grated lemon rind
1 tablespoon flour	¼ teaspoon salt
3 egg yolks	2 tablespoons butter, melted
⅓ cup lemon juice	3 egg whites
	1 cup milk

Blend the sugar with flour. Add egg yolks, lemon juice, rind, salt and butter. Fold in whites of eggs and add milk. Pour in unbaked pie crust. Bake in moderate oven.

SCHNA-DAWLER PIE

Many years ago when my parents lived on a farm my mother had a woman to help her with the house work. The woman baked pies and when there was any dough left she baked the following pie. The woman lived in a valley called "Schna-Dawl" so we always called this pie Schna-Dawler Pie.
—*Mrs. Paul Mattern*

2 tablespoons sugar	Cinnamon
2 tablespoons flour	¼ teaspoon vanilla
¾ cup milk	1 tablespoon butter

Mix the sugar, flour, milk and vanilla. Pour into unbaked pie crusts. Dot with butter. Sprinkle cinnamon on top. Bake at 350° until crust is brown and filling is thick.

CAKE PIE

Cake Pie has been a favorite in my husband's family for generations.
—*Mrs. Roy G. Miller*

Juice:

½ teaspoon soda	½ cup molasses
1 cup hot water	½ teaspoon vanilla
½ cup granulated sugar	1 egg

Cake:

1 cup sugar	½ cup milk
¼ cup butter and lard	1½ cups flour
1 egg	½ teaspoon soda

Prepare two unbaked pie shells using your favorite recipe. Mix the soda for the juice in hot water. Then, combine all the ingredients for the juice and pour into the two pie shells. The cake is made next by mixing the sugar, butter and lard, and egg and adding milk, flour and soda. Drop the batter by the spoonful into the juice. Place the pies in a cold oven and set the temperature at 375°. Test after ½ hour with a toothpick. Pie top should be brown.

CHOCOLATE CUSTARD PIE
—Mrs. J.W. Herr

3 tablespoons grated chocolate or cocoa	4 egg yolks, well beaten
1 cup milk	1 teaspoon vanilla
¾ cup granulated sugar	4 egg whites, beaten stiff
	4 tablespoons sugar

Boil chocolate and milk until mixture begins to thicken. Add granulated sugar and egg yolks, bring to boil but do not boil. Take off stove and add vanilla. Pour in 1 large and 1 small baked pie shell. Place in oven and bake until pie rises firm. Spread top with mixture of stiff egg whites and sugar. Brown in oven.

67

PEACH TART

4 peaches ¼ **cup cream**
½ cup sugar **1 egg**

Cut peaches into halves or quarters and fill unbaked pie shell. Mix sugar, cream and egg. Pour over peaches and bake.

LEPP COOKIES

Wednesday was market day on our farm, and because my bedroom was directly over the kitchen I always awoke, on Wednesdays, to the delectable aroma of "just-out-of-the-oven" lepp cookies which my mother baked for market.

She would start at 4 o'clock in the morning —first firing up the cook-stove which stood in the center of the kitchen, and then mixing the ingredients in a huge white dishpan, using a big wooden spoon to stir.

Her recipe, "Aunt Barbara's Lepp Cakes," was from the handwritten notebook of her favorite recipes, but she no longer referred to this. Her practiced hand knew just how much of each ingredient was needed and her "guess-work" always worked! She would first bake a test cookie on a tin pie pan and sometimes she needed to add more flour, but most times it was soft and chewy—just right.

The following recipe is not the one my mother used, but is far more accurate and is very delicious, as well.
—Mrs. Conrad Graybill

1¾ cups shortening	1 tablespoon baking soda
2 pounds brown sugar	6 tablespoons baking powder
3 eggs	1 teaspoon cream of tartar
1 pint sour cream	½ teaspoon salt
8½ cups flour	

Cream shortening; add sugar; cream again. Add eggs, mix well and add milk. Sift all dry ingredients and add. (More flour may be needed.) Bake at 350° for approximately 10 to 12 minutes.

HARD GINGER COOKIES

A 200-year-old recipe once the proud possession of the late Mrs. Jake Hellman, whose forebears brought it from abroad.

1 cup dark molasses	1 teaspoon baking soda dissolved in 1 tablespoon vinegar
1 cup lard	
1 cup brown sugar	6 cups sifted flour
1 egg	Cinnamon sugar
2 teaspoons ginger	

In a double boiler melt molasses, lard and sugar. Cool and add egg, ginger and baking soda. Add flour and roll out very thin. Cut and sprinkle with cinnamon sugar. Bake 7 to 10 minutes at 375°.

MOLASSES COOKIES

—Amelia S. Zimmerman

2 cups lard	2 teaspoons baking
2 cups molasses	soda
	Flour

Mix lard, molasses and baking soda which has been dissolved in a little bit of water. Add enough flour to make batter easy to handle. Roll thin and cut with a cookie cutter.

SOFT CREAM JUMBLES

My mother used this recipes to make cookies for my children. I use it now for my grandchildren—they love them as much as my sons did.
—Mrs. Eugene Zerbe

½ cup shortening (part butter for flavor)	½ teaspoon baking powder
1½ cups of sugar	1 teaspoon vinegar
2 eggs	1 cup milk
3½ cups of flour	½ teaspoon baking soda
½ teaspoon salt	1 teaspoon vanilla

Cream together butter or margarine with sugar, add eggs. Sift flour, salt and powder together and blend with creamed mixture. Mix vinegar and milk and add with soda to the mixture. Add vanilla and drop by teaspoonful on baking sheets. You can make them any size you want. I usually bake half the batch with cinnamon and sugar sprinkled on top and the other half plain. Then I ice with a butter icing (for Christmas, I sprinkle colored sugar on top). Bake at 350° till golden. *Makes about 5 dozen cookies.*

MICHIGAN ROCKS

A Christmas delicacy.
—Grace Groff

3 cups flour	1 teaspoon baking soda
1½ cups light brown sugar	2 teaspoons vanilla
½ pound butter	¾ pound chopped dates
3 eggs	½ pound chopped walnuts
½ teaspoon cinnamon	

Mix the first seven ingredients, reserving a little flour to sprinkle on the dates and walnuts, and cream 3 to 4 minutes with an electric mixer. Stir in dates and walnuts. Drop by teaspoonful on cookie sheet and bake at 350° for 10 to 15 minutes or until brown.

NANNY'S COCONUT DROPS

These were always baked for Christmas and were served with homemade wine in pretty stem glasses. Whenever townspeople dropped in, we ran to the attic and filled our glass dish. The drops were stored in a huge basket wrapped in a snow-white linen cloth.
—Mrs. John H. Brown

½ pound butter	1 pound flour
1 pound sugar	2 teaspoons baking
Meat of 1 large	powder
coconut	

Cream butter and sugar. Grind the coconut meat coarsely in a meat grinder and stir into mixture. Mix in flour and baking powder and stir into creamed mixture. Drop by teaspoonful on cookie sheet and bake at 375° for 12 minutes or until tester comes out clean.

MAMA'S FUDGE CAKE

As a child, when we went to our Sunday School picnic, everyone wanted a piece of this cake and there was never enough for everyone and so "first there, first served." This was one of the highlights of the picnic supper and

members of the band could not play a proper concert without slices.
—Mrs. John H. Brown

2 cups brown sugar	2 cups flour
½ cup butter	1 teaspoon baking soda
2 eggs	2 tablespoons cocoa
½ cup hot water	

Mix the sugar and butter and add the rest of the ingredients. Pour batter into two 9-inch pie pans. Bake at 350° for 25 minutes. This cake will not rise very much and the layers will not look right. Don't be alarmed, the cake will look beautiful and taste good. The following filling will enhance the cake immeasurably.

Filling:

⅔ cup brown sugar	2 tablespoons cornstarch dissolved in ½ cup cold water
1 tablespoon cocoa dissolved in 1 cup boiling water	Butter
	Vanilla

Mix and boil the first three ingredients. Add butter and vanilla, let stand a few minutes and spread.

OLD GERMAN SPICE CAKE

2 cups brown
sugar
¾ cup lard
3 egg yolks
1½ teaspoons
ground cloves
1 teaspoon
baking soda

1½ teaspoons
allspice
2 cups sifted
flour
1 cup cold water
3 egg whites,
beaten stiffly
Raisins or nuts
(optional)

Mix sugar and lard. Add egg yolks, cloves, allspice, flour and water. Fold in egg whites and add raisins or nuts, if desired.

MORAVIAN SUGAR CAKE

—Mrs. Willis H. Bucher

1 cup mashed
potatoes
⅔ cup shortening
½ cup sugar
1 heaping
tablespoon salt
2 eggs

1 yeast cake
½ cup lukewarm
water
1 cup scalded
milk
7 cups flour
Butter

In a bowl, mix potatoes, shortening, sugar, salt and eggs. Cream well. Dissolve yeast in water and add to lukewarm milk and then to mixture. Add flour, leave overnight. Knead, put on board and knead a little more. Put in bowl and let rise, rub top with butter. Put in aluminum cookie sheet and let rise for about 1½ hours. Punch finger holes on top and fill with butter. Top with the following and bake at 400° for 15 to 20 minutes.

Topping:

1 pound brown sugar	Butter
1 cup flour	Cinnamon

Mix the first three ingredients to make crumbs. Spread over top of cake and sprinkle with cinnamon.

BLACK WALNUT CAKE

—*Mrs. Viola Bricker*

½ cup butter	¾ cup cold water
1½ cups sugar	1 cup chopped
1 teaspoon baking powder	black walnuts
2 cups flour	4 egg whites

Cream butter and gradually add the sugar, creaming until light and fluffy. Sift together the baking powder and flour, add it alternately with the water to the creamed mixture. Carefully fold in the nuts and then the beaten egg whites. Bake in two 8-inch layer pans for 30-35 minutes at 350°. Frost with a walnut frosting.

FUNNEL CAKES

*Wonderful to make on a cool, fall evening.
Eat with molasses or syrup and country-fried
sausage.*
—Mrs. John H. Brown

2 cups milk	2 teaspoons
3 eggs	baking powder
4 cups flour	2 tablespoons
½ teaspoon salt	sugar

Beat eggs and milk together. Add remaining
ingredients and mix. Drop in the shape of a
large coil through a funnel with a long handle
and fry in deep fat. Start in the center of the
pan and pour in circles to the sides of the pan.

DEVIL'S FOOD CAKE

2 cups brown sugar (scant if granulated)	½ cup cocoa
	1½ teaspoons baking powder
1 cup butter and lard	1 teaspoon baking soda
3 egg yolks	½ cup thick milk
1 teaspoon vanilla	½ cup hot water
2 cups flour	3 egg whites

Cream sugar and shortening, add yolks and
vanilla. Sift dry ingredients together four
times and add alternately with milk and then
water. Fold in beaten egg whites.

76

BLACK JOE CAKE

1 cup brown sugar
1 cup granulated sugar
½ cup lard
1 cup thick milk
½ cup cocoa mixed with ½ cup boiling water
1 teaspoon baking soda
1 teaspoon vanilla
3½ cups sifted flour
Salt

Mix sugar and lard; add milk. Mix cocoa and soda and add to mixture. Then add vanilla, flour and a pinch of salt.

DORCAS CAKE

—*Mrs. Simon Nunemaker*

1 pound raisins	½ teaspoon
½ cup shortening	nutmeg
2 cups sugar	1 tablespoon
1 cup cold water	baking soda
1 teaspoon	1 cup cold water
cinnamon	4 cups flour
½ teaspoon cloves	

Stew raisins for 12 minutes in 2 cups of water. Let cool. In a bowl mix shortening, sugar, water, cinnamon, cloves, nutmeg and baking soda. Mix in raisins and add cold water. Beat in flour and pour in cake pan. Bake for 40 to 45 minutes at 350°. For a slightly lighter cake, add 3 eggs. This recipe can also be used for cupcakes or bars. Spread batter on floured cookie sheets with sides. Bake 15 to 20 minutes. When cool, ice with thin confectioners' sugar icing. Cut into bars.

ICE CREAM CAKE

—*Mary Harsh*

1 cup butter	1 cup milk
2 cups sugar	3½ cups flour
2 teaspoons	8 egg whites
baking powder	1 teaspoon
¼ teaspoon salt	vanilla

Cream butter and add sugar, baking powder, salt and milk. Then add flour and beat.

Add whipped egg whites and beat again; flavor with vanilla. Bake in three jelly tins in hot oven and when cold spread each layer with melted chocolate. When cold ice with the following.

Icing:

2 cups granulated   Vanilla
  sugar
1 cup cream or
  rich milk

Mix and boil sugar and cream until it forms a soft ball when dropped in water. Remove from fire and add vanilla. Let set for a few minutes before starting to beat. Beat until creamy. Put on cake layers and spread with chocolate.

1—2—3—4 CAKE

—Mrs. John H. Brown

1 cup butter   3 cups flour
1 box   2 teaspoons
  confectioners'   baking powder
  sugar   1⅓ cups milk
4 egg yolks   4 egg whites,
                              stiffly beaten

Cream butter, sugar and egg yolks. Gradually stir in flour, baking powder, milk and finally egg whites. Beat thoroughly. Pour cake batter into two 9-inch cake pans and bake at 350° for 20 to 25 minutes.

FUDGE FROSTING

—Mrs. R. L. Wiggins

¼ cup butter (⅛ pound)	1¾ cup sifted confectioners' sugar
½ cup cocoa	
¼ cup water	½ teaspoon vanilla
Pinch of salt	

Melt butter, stir in cocoa and water. Cook over low flame until thick and well blended. Remove from heat, add salt. Add sifted sugar in small portions, mixing thoroughly after each addition. Add vanilla.

APPLE ROLL

I am a 15-year-old farm girl. This recipe came into our family when my mother was a little girl. A hired boy who worked for my grandparents brought it from his home in Mifflin County. It has been a family recipe ever since. We use it as a cold dessert with milk.
—*Barbara L. Stoltzfus*

2½ cups flour	3 teaspoons lard
½ teaspoon salt	1 egg
2 tablespoons sugar	½ cup sweet milk
4 teaspoons baking powder	Apples

Combine flour, salt, sugar, baking powder, lard, egg and milk to make the dough. Roll out the dough as for a pie. Cut apples in thin slices until there is enough to cover the dough. Sprinkle with cinnamon and roll up lengthwise. Cut the roll into pieces about 2-inches long. Pour the following syrup over slices and bake at 350° for about half an hour.

Syrup:

2 cups granulated sugar	1 cup water

Cook the sugar in the water until the sugar is dissolved.

HUCKLEBERRY MUFFINS

—Mrs. Lloyd K. LeFever

2 cups flour	1 egg, beaten
4 teaspoons baking powder	2 tablespoons melted butter
½ teaspoon salt	1 cup milk
4 tablespoons sugar	1 cup huckleberries

Sift flour; measure and reserve 3 tablespoons to dust berries. To remaining flour add baking powder, salt and sugar. Sift again. Add egg and butter to milk and combine with dry ingredients. Fold in berries. Drop by the spoonful into greased muffin pans. Bake at 400° for 25 minutes. *Makes 12 to 15 muffins.*

KRUMMEL KUCHEN

This prize-winning Pennsylvania Dutch recipe has been in the family for many years. It was made especially in farm homes and kept on hand at all times. In those days tramps came along almost every day. This is one cake they all enjoyed.
—Mrs. Loran Wenrich

2 cups flour	½ cup butter
1½ cups granulated sugar	2 eggs, well beaten
2 teaspoons baking powder	½ cup milk
¼ teaspoon salt	Few drops vanilla

Sift dry ingredients together, work in butter. Reserve ½ cup of this mixture. Add eggs, milk and vanilla and beat well. Pour into a buttered and floured 9-inch cake pan, top with the reserved mixture. Sprinkle with cinnamon if desired. Bake in moderate oven, 350-375°, for 50 minutes.

COFFEE CAKE

This gets hard in a day or two and rightly so because they were meant for dunking. They are particularly good when soft—just after baking.
—Mrs. John H. Brown

4 cups flour	½ cup lard
1 teaspoon baking soda	Buttermilk Granulated sugar
1½ cups brown sugar	

Add enough buttermilk to keep dough together and press into pans. Sprinkle with granulated sugar and put into 8-inch pie pan. Bake at 375° until toothpick comes out clean.

HONEY CAKES

1 quart honey	4 egg yolks, well beaten
½ cup butter	
2 scant tablespoons baking soda	2 pounds 5 ounces of bread flour
	4 egg whites

Boil the honey and skim it. Add butter and let cool until mixture is lukewarm, then add baking soda dissolved in a little warm water. Add egg yolks, then flour. Beat egg whites until stiff and fold in. Keep cookie batter in the refrigerator for about 1½ hours before baking. Drop by the teaspoonful on cookie sheet and bake for 10 minutes at 375°. *Makes 200 cookies.*

AUNT IDA'S SPONGE CAKE

Whenever we went to Aunt Ida's farm, we would go to her ground cellar and get a piece of this cake from the pie safe.
—*Mrs. John H. Brown*

1 cup eggs	Pinch of salt
1 cup sugar	1 teaspoon vanilla
1 cup flour	

Mix eggs and sugar and beat until thick. Add flour, salt and vanilla. Bake at 350° for 30 minutes in a sponge-cake pan. Don't worry about not adding a liquid. Mother also used this recipe for strawberry shortcake.

HOT MILK SPONGE

—*Julia L. Glackin*

4 eggs	1 heaping teaspoon
2 cups sugar	baking powder
2 cups flour	extract
	1 cup boiling milk

Mix eggs and sugar and beat well with a spoon. Add flour and extract. This mixture will be very stiff. Stir in the milk. Now the mixture is very thin but do not thicken. Bake in a large loaf pan with a tube in a slow oven (300°) for ¾ of an hour.

CINNAMON FLAT

1 cup brown sugar	1 cup milk
1 tablespoon butter	Salt
2 teaspoons baking powder	2 teaspoons cinnamon
2 cups flour	½ cup brown sugar

Beat sugar and butter. Sift baking powder and flour and add with milk and salt. Pour into square pan. Mix cinnamon and sugar and sprinkle on top. Bake

GRANDMA'S CINNAMON FLOP

—*Mrs. John H. Brown*

1 cup granulated sugar	2 teaspoons baking powder
1 tablespoon butter	1 cup brown sugar
1 cup milk	¼ pound butter
2 cups flour	Cinnamon
¼ teaspoon salt	Nutmeg

Cream butter and mix with sugar. Add milk, flour, salt and baking powder. Pour into a greased 8-inch pie pan. Mix remaining ingredients to form crumbs. Divide evenly over batter. Bake for 20 minutes at 425°.

FASNACHTS

Grandma always said, "If you don't make doughnuts on Fasnacht Day (Shrove Tuesday) your house roof will blow off before the year is past." These are the doughnuts we made.
—*Miss Sue Etta Nolt*

2 cups warm potato water	1 cup sugar
2 cups warm mashed potatoes	3 tablespoons butter
2 tablespoons sugar	¼ teaspoon salt
2 cakes dry yeast	1¼ cups sifted flour
1 egg, well beaten	

Combine 1 cup potato water, mashed potatoes, and sugar. Dissolve yeast in remaining potato water and add to other ingredients. Let the mixture rise until bubbles burst on top. Combine the egg, sugar, butter and salt. Gradually add flour to make a soft dough, not too stiff. Add this batter to the yeast dough and knead well. Place in well-greased covered bowl to rise for 1½ hours. Roll the dough out on a floured board to ¼-inch thickness, cut with a doughnut cutter, and let rise for an additional hour. Drop the uncooked doughnuts in hot lard. Bake at 375°. Remove the doughnuts when they are brown.

DOUGHNUTS

—Mrs. Lloyd K. LeFever

2 eggs	½ teaspoon
1 cup sugar	nutmeg
2 tablespoons	½ teaspoon salt
melted butter	1 cup sour milk
5 cups flour	mixed with:
3 teaspoons	1 teaspoon
baking powder	baking soda

Beat the eggs and add sugar and butter. Mix the flour, baking powder, nutmeg and salt and add to egg mixture. Add mixture of sour milk and soda. Roll out on floured board. Cut with a doughnut cutter. Drop into hot fat, 375°, brown on one side, turn and brown on the other side. Drain. Shake in bag of confectioners' sugar.

KNEE PATCHES

Long ago, this was a popular treat for weddings or special feasts. A tea towel was used to cover the knee and the dough was stretched over the knee until very thin and then fried in deep fat. They are delicious as a dessert with lots of fresh fruit.
—*Mrs. Lloyd K. LeFever*

3 eggs	**4 cups flour**
1 cup cream	**½ teaspoon salt**

Beat eggs and add cream. Sift flour and salt together and stir into egg mixture to make a soft dough. Take a piece of dough about the size of a large marble and roll as thinly as possible. Fry in deep fat until delicately brown. Drain and shake in a bag of powdered sugar. Makes 24 to 30 patches.

INDEX